Third Earth

A New Blessed Hope

by

Ivor Forbes

RoseDog Books
PITTSBURGH, PENNSYLVANIA 15238

RoseDog Books
585 Alpha Drive, Suite 103
Pittsburgh, PA 15238
Visit our website at *www.rosedogbookstore.com*

ISBN: 979-8-88729-403-2
eISBN: 979-8-88729-903-7

The Lord God Almighty has hidden great mysteries within his holy word.

 4And my speech and my preaching was not with enticing words of man's wisdom, but in demonstration of the Spirit and of power:

5 That your faith should not stand in the wisdom of men, but in the power of God. 6Howbeit we speak wisdom among them that are perfect: yet not the wisdom of this world, nor of the princes of this world, that come to nought:

7 But we speak the wisdom of God in a mystery, *even* the hidden *wisdom,* which God ordained before the world unto our glory:

8 Which none of the princes of this world knew: for had they known *it,* they would not have crucified the Lord of glory.

9 But as it is written, Eye hath not seen, nor ear heard, neither have entered into the heart of man, the things which God hath prepared for them that love him.

10 But God hath revealed *them* unto us by his Spirit: for the Spirit searcheth all things, yea, the deep things of God.

11 For what man knoweth the things of a man, save the spirit of man which is in him? even so the things of God knoweth no man, but the Spirit of God.

12 Now we have received, not the spirit of the world, but the spirit which is of God; that we might know the things that are freely given to us of God.

13 <u>Which things also we speak, not in the words which man's wisdom teacheth, but which the Holy Ghost teacheth; comparing spiritual things with spiritual.</u> 14<u>But the natural man receiveth not the things of the Spirit of God: for they are foolishness unto him: neither can he know</u> *them*<u>, because they are spiritually discerned.</u>

15 <u>But he that is spiritual judgeth all things, yet he himself is judged of no man.</u> 16<u>For who hath known the mind of the Lord, that he may instruct him? But we have the mind of Christ.</u> (1cor2:4-16) *It is* <u>the glory of God to conceal a thing: but the honour of kings</u> *is* <u>to search out a matter.</u> (Prov 25:2).

I will not turn aside from his way. As a BABIC (Born-Again Believer in Christ)® who follows the Way of the Lord of Holiness (<u>And an highway shall be there, and a way, and it shall be called The way of holiness; the unclean shall not pass over it; but it</u> *shall be* <u>for those: the wayfaring men, though</u> <u>fools, shall not err</u> *therein.* Isaiah 35:8.) I am a student of the Holy Spirit of God. It is my belief that *God the Heavenly Father will reveal the mysteries of his word to those who he inscribed into the Lamb's book of life, chosen and anointed with his Holy Spirit. These chosen ones have been baptized by water and by the Holy Spirit and are awaiting their appointing or are already appointed in their ministry/ministries God had predestined for them.

I am no theologian, Apostle, Prophet, preacher, nor teacher. Therefore, everything I share is purely speculative. It is my belief that I am under the unction of the Holy Spirit to share that which He has taught me and from the things I've learned through investing quality devotional time reading God's word and praying.

As per the word anyone who has been baptized by God's Holy Spirit is anointed. (<u>But ye have an unction from the Holy One, and ye know all</u> <u>things. But the anointing which ye have received of him abideth in you, and ye need not that any man teach you: but as the same anointing teacheth you of all</u> <u>things, and is truth, and is no lie, and even as it hath taught you, ye shall abide in him.</u> 1John:20,27). I write this because even though my comprehension doesn't come from the instruction of men, I want to make it clear that the understanding that I do have I acquired from the Holy Spirit who is available to all BABICs®. God gives his wisdom to all BABICs® without being stingy. (<u>If any of you lack wisdom, let him ask of God, that giveth to all</u> *men* <u>liberally, and upbraideth not; and it shall be given</u> <u>him.</u> James1:5) God is the most High God of gods. There is nothing or no one above Him. His glory is from everlasting to everlasting, and His wisdom is (<u>But the wisdom that is from above is first pure, then peaceable, gentle,</u> *and* <u>easy to be intreated, full of mercy and good fruits, without partiality, and without hypocrisy.</u>

18 And the fruit of righteousness is sown in peace of them that make peace. James3:17,18) Also, (Who is a wise man and endued with knowledge among you? let him shew out of a good conversation his works with meekness of wisdom. James3:13)

Most Christians already know of the blessed hope. (But I will not have you to be ignorant, brethren, concerning them which are asleep that ye sorrow not, even as others which have no hope.

14 For if we believe that Jesus died and rose again, even so them also which sleep in Jesus will God bring with him.

15 For this we say unto you by the word of the Lord, that we which are alive *and* remain unto the coming of the Lord shall not prevent them which are asleep.

16 For the Lord himself shall descend from heaven with a shout, with the voice of the archangel, and with the trump of God: and the dead in Christ shall rise first:

17 Then we which are alive *and* remain shall be caught up together with them in the clouds, to meet the Lord in the air: and so shall we ever be with the Lord.

18 Wherefore comfort one another with these words. 1Thessalonians4:13–18) Also, Christians are aware that heaven and earth shall pass away and God will make everything new. (But the day of the Lord will come as a thief in the night; in the which the heavens shall pass away with a great noise, and the elements shall melt with fervent heat, the earth also and the works that are therein shall be burned up.

11 *Seeing then that* all these things shall be dissolved, what manner *of persons* ought ye to be in *all* holy conversation and godliness,

12 Looking for and hasting unto the coming of the day of God, wherein the heavens being on fire shall be dissolved, and the elements shall melt with fervent heat? 13Nevertheless we, according to his promise, look for new heavens and a new earth, wherein dwelleth righteousness. And I saw a new heaven and a new earth: for the first heaven and the first earth were passed away; and there was no more sea. And he that sat upon the throne said, Behold, I make all things new. And he said unto me, Write: for these words are true and faithful. 2Peter3:10-13; Revelation21:1;5). Not too many Christians are aware of or believe that new Jerusalem will descend from heaven upon third Earth (And I saw a new heaven and a new earth: for the first heaven and the first earth were passed away; and there was no more sea.

2 And I John saw the holy city, new Jerusalem, coming down from God out of heaven, prepared as a bride adorned for her husband.

3 <u>And I heard a great voice out of heaven saying, Behold, the tabernacle of God</u> *is* <u>with</u> <u>men, and he will</u> <u>dwell with them, and they shall be his people, and God himself shall</u> <u>be with them,</u> *and be* <u>their God.</u> Revelation 21:1-3) Naturally, to those who don't know, the question to ask should be, "So what's first Earth?" (<u>And saying,</u> <u>Where is the</u> <u>promise of his coming? for since the fathers fell asleep, all things continue as</u> *they were* <u>from the</u> <u>beginning of the creation.</u> 2 Peter 3:4) The beginning of creation, not the beginning of restoration.

The story of first Earth starts at in the beginning, not in Genesis1:1, but in (<u>In the beginning was the</u> <u>Word, and the Word was with God, and the</u> <u>Word was God.</u> **2**<u>The same was in the beginning with God.</u> John1:1,2).

The enigma of God is this: He is Spirit God *is* a Spirit, and they that worship him must worship *him* in spirit and in truth. (John 4:24), The God Father of Spirits (<u>Let the LORD,</u> <u>the God of the spirits of all</u> <u>flesh, set a man over the congregation,</u> <u>Furthermore we have</u> <u>had fathers of our flesh which corrected</u> *us,* <u>and we gave</u> *them* <u>reverence: shall we not</u> <u>much rather be in subjection unto the Father of spirits, and live?</u> Numbers 27:16, Hebrews 12:9). He is three persons in one being which is called the Godhead. God the Father, God the Word/Son, and God the Holy Spirit. God also has a soul. (<u>Your new</u> <u>moons and your ap-</u> <u>pointed feasts my soul hateth: they are a trouble unto me; I am</u> <u>weary to bear</u> *them.* <u>Shall I not visit for these</u> *things*<u>? saith the LORD: shall not my soul</u> <u>be avenged on such a nation as this?</u> Isaiah1:14, Jerimiah 5:29) It is my belief that there is a hierarchy within the Godhead even though all three are equally God. God the Father is Supreme. The Holy Spirit glorifies not himself, but the Son and the Father. In due time, when the Son has subdued and conquered all things, He will submit to God so that God is supreme over all. (<u>Who is the image of the invisible God, the firstborn of</u> <u>every creature:</u> **16**<u>For by him were all things created,</u> <u>that are in heaven, and that are in</u> <u>earth, visible and invisible, whether</u> *they be* <u>thrones, or dominions, or</u> <u>principalities, or</u> <u>powers: all things were created by him, and for him:</u>

17<u>And he is before all things, and</u> <u>by him all things consist.</u>

18 <u>And he is the head of the body, the church: who is the beginning, the firstborn from</u> <u>the dead; that</u> <u>in all</u> *things* <u>he might have the preeminence.</u>

19 <u>For it pleased</u> *the Father* <u>that in him should all fulness dwell;</u>

20 <u>And, having made peace through the blood of his cross, by him to reconcile all things</u> <u>unto himself;</u> <u>by him,</u> *I say,* <u>whether</u> *they be* <u>things in earth, or things in heaven.</u> <u>Then</u> *cometh* <u>the end, when he shall have</u> <u>delivered up the kingdom to God, even the</u> <u>Father; when he shall have put down all rule and all authority</u> <u>and power.</u>

25 For he must reign, till he hath put all enemies under his feet.

26 The last enemy *that* shall be destroyed *is* death.

27 For he hath put all things under his feet. But when he saith all things are put under *him, it is* manifest that he is excepted, which did put all things under him. **28**And when all things shall be subdued unto him, then shall the Son also himself be subject unto him that put all things under him, that God may be all in all. Who, being in the form of God, thought it not robbery to be equal with God:

7 But made himself of no reputation, and took upon him the form of a servant, and was made in the likeness of men:

8 And being found in fashion as a man, he humbled himself, and became obedient unto death, even the death of the cross.

9 Wherefore God also hath highly exalted him, and given him a name which is above every name:

10 That at the name of Jesus every knee should bow, of *things* in heaven, and *things* in earth, and *things* under the earth;

11 And *that* every tongue should confess that Jesus Christ *is* Lord, to the glory of God the Father. Colossians 1:15-20; 1 Corinthians 15:24–28; Phillipians 2:6–11).

In addition to the Godhead another being co-existed with the Godhead and his name is Melchizedek, the king of Salem. For this Melchisedec, king of

Salem, priest of the most high God, who met Abraham returning from the

slaughter of the kings, and blessed him;

2 To whom also Abraham gave a tenth part of all; first being by interpretation King of righteousness, and after that also King of Salem, which is, King of peace;

3 Without father, without mother, without descent, having neither beginning of days, nor end of life; but made like unto the Son of God; abideth a priest continually. **4**Now consider how great this man *was,* unto whom even the patriarch Abraham gave the tenth of the spoils. Hebrews 7:1–4) He was called Priest of God Most High. The Godhead and Melchizedek always existed, were never created and are immortal.

The first of God's works, who is personified as feminine, is wisdom. (But we speak the wisdom of God in a mystery, *even* the hidden *wisdom,* which God ordained before the world unto our glory: The LORD possessed me in the beginning of his way, before his works of old.

23 I was set up from everlasting, from the beginning, or ever the earth was. **24**When *there were* no depths, I was brought forth; when *there were* no fountains abounding with water.

25 <u>Before the mountains were settled, before the hills was I brought forth:</u>

26 <u>While as yet he had not made the earth, nor the fields, nor the highest part of the dust of the world.</u>

27 <u>When he prepared the heavens, I *was* there: when he set a compass upon the face of the depth:</u>

28 <u>When he established the clouds above: when he strengthened the fountains of the deep:</u>

29 <u>When he gave to the sea his decree, that the waters should not pass his commandment: when he appointed the foundations of the earth:</u>

30 <u>Then I was by him, *as* one brought up *with him*: and I was daily *his* delight, rejoicing always before him;</u> 1 Corinthians 2:7; Proverbs 8:22–31) According to the word, God created Wisdom first. It is my belief that the sons of God (i.e., Angels) and stars were present as God created first Earth and the Lamb's Book of Life was also already in existence.

<u>Where wast thou when I laid the foundations of the earth? declare, if thou hast understanding.</u>

5 <u>Who hath laid the measures thereof, if thou knowest? or who hath stretched the line upon it?</u>

6 <u>Whereupon are the foundations thereof fastened? or who laid the corner stone thereof;</u> **7**<u>When the morning stars sang together, and all the sons of God shouted for joy? According as he hath chosen us in him before the foundation of the world, that we should be holy and without blame before him in love: And all that dwell upon the earth shall worship him, whose names are not written in the book of life of the Lamb slain from the foundation of the world. The beast that thou sawest was, and is not; and shall ascend out of the bottomless pit, and go into perdition: and they that dwell on the earth shall wonder, whose names were not written in the book of life from the foundation of the world, when they behold the beast that was, and is not, and yet is.</u> Job 38:4–7; Ephesians 1:4; Revelation 13:8, 17:8)

(Genesis1:1) All of these events happened during in the beginning prior to his brings me to

<u>In the beginning God created the heaven and the earth.</u>

Genesis1:1. <u>Can any hide himself in secret places that I shall not see him?</u>

<u>saith the LORD. Do not I fill heaven and earth? saith the LORD. By the word of the LORD were the heavens made; and all the host of them by the breath of his mouth.</u> **1**<u>In the beginning was the Word, and the Word was with God, and the Word was God.</u>

2 <u>The same was in the beginning with God.</u>

3 <u>All things were made by him; and without him was not any thing made that was made.</u>

4 <u>In him was life; and the life was the light of men.</u> **15**<u>Who is the image of the invisible God, the first-born of every creature:</u>

16 For by him were all things created, that are in heaven, and that are in earth, visible and invisible, whether *they be* thrones, or dominions, or principalities, or powers: all things were created by him, and for him:

17 And he is before all things, and by him all things consist.

18 And he is the head of the body, the church: who is the beginning, the firstborn from the dead; that in all *things* he might have the preeminence.

19 For it pleased *the Father* that in him should all fulness dwell; Jerimiah 23:24; Psalms 33:6; John 1:1–4; Colossians 1:15–20) The Word is Jesus, and he existed in the beginning with God the Father and God the Holy Spirit. The term *was* can be replaced with *became*, and it doesn't lose its meaning, rather it magnifies it. (1In the beginning was the Word, and the Word was with God, and the Word was God.

2 The same was in the beginning with God.

3 All things were made by him; and without him was not any thing made that was made.

4 In him was life; and the life was the light of men. John1:1-4;

23 I beheld the earth, and, lo, *it was* without form, and void; and the heavens, and they *had* no light. Jerimiah 4:23 **2** And the earth was without form, and void; and darkness *was* upon the face of the deep. And the Spirit of God moved upon the face of the waters. Genesis1:2. If I substitute *was* for *became*, scripture reads as follows: I beheld the Earth and lo, it became without form and void and darkness became upon the face of the deep. According to the revised scripture we can deduce that something happened in order to cause first Earth to be in such a devastated state.

 It is written (Thus saith the LORD, The heaven *is* my throne, and the earth *is* my footstool: where *is* the house that ye build unto me? and where *is* the place of my rest? 18For thus saith the LORD that created the heavens; God himself that formed the earth and made it; he hath established it, he created it not in vain, he formed it to be inhabited: I *am* the LORD; and *there is* none else. Isaiah 66:1; 45:18). Based on Isaiah 45:18, I believe that life existed on other planets during the reign of first Earth. I also believe that first Earth was inhabited by mankind, not Adam and Eve. When God receded the flood waters from the Earth and Noah exited the Ark with his family and the animals God said to him (1And God blessed Noah and his sons, and said unto them, Be fruitful, and multiply, and replenish the earth. Genesis 9:1) Now, it makes sense that God would tell Noah and his family to replenish the Earth because only eight souls survived the flood. (20Which sometime were disobedient, when once the longsuffering of God waited in the days of Noah, while the ark was a preparing, wherein few, that is, eight souls were saved by water.; 5And spared not the old world, but saved Noah the eighth *person*, a preacher of righteousness, bringing in the flood upon the world of the ungodly; 1 Peter3:20; 2Peter2:5). It should raise an eyebrow as to why God said 28And God blessed them, and God said unto them, Be fruitful, and multiply, and replenish the earth, and subdue it: and have dominion over the fish of the sea, and over the fowl of the air, and over every living thing that moveth upon the earth. (Genesis1:28) Why would God bless man, i.e. humanity (male and female), and tell them to replenish the Earth on the sixth day of creation? Let's not forget that man, i.e., Adam, was formed from the dust after the seventh day in which the Lord rested from all of his work. 3And God blessed the seventh day, and sanctified it: because that in it he had rested from all his work which God created and made. 7And the LORD God formed man *of* the dust of the ground, and breathed into his nostrils the breath of life; and man became a living soul. Genesis2:3,7).

What was first earth like? It is my belief that second earth or our earth is very similar to first Earth very similar to first Earth which had Eden, nations, people commerce, cities, kingdoms, precious gemstones and metals etc…

When God created his heavenly hosts, he ascribed ranks to them in their first estate. For example, King Abaddon's kingdom is the Bottomless Pit, i.e. the Abyss (11And they had a king over them, *which is* the angel of the bottomless pit, whose name in the Hebrew tongue *is* Abaddon, but in the Greek tongue hath *his* name Apollyon. Revelation9:11). Lucifer, in his first estate, was the morning star, son of the dawn and the anointed cherub that covereth (12How art thou fallen from heaven, O Lucifer, son of the morning! *how* art thou cut down to the ground, which didst weaken the nations!

14 Thou *art* the anointed cherub that covereth; and I have set thee *so*: thou wast upon the holy mountain of God; thou hast walked up and down in the midst of the stones of fire. 16By the multitude of thy merchandise they have filled the midst of thee with violence, and thou hast sinned: therefore I will cast thee as profane out of the mountain of God: and I will destroy thee, O covering cherub, from the midst of the stones of fire.

Isaiah 14:12; Ezekiel 28:14,16)

It is written (70As he spake by the mouth of his holy prophets, which have been since the world began: Luke1:70) If this is second Earth then according to the word prophets existed on first Earth also. Here are further indications of a first Earth (12How art thou fallen from heaven, O Lucifer, son of the morning! *how* art thou cut down to the ground, which didst weaken the nations!

13 For thou hast said in thine heart, I will ascend into heaven, I will exalt my throne above the stars

of God: I will sit also upon the mount of the congregation, in the sides of the north:

14 I will ascend above the heights of the clouds; I will be like the most High.

15 Yet thou shalt be brought down to hell, to the sides of the pit.

16They that see thee shall narrowly look upon thee, *and* consider thee, *saying, Is* this the man that made the earth to tremble, that did shake kingdoms;

17 *That* made the world as a wilderness, and destroyed the cities thereof; *that* opened not the house of his prisoners?

18 All the kings of the nations, *even* all of them, lie in glory, every one in his own house.

19 But thou art cast out of thy grave like an abominable branch, *and as* the raiment of those that are slain, thrust through with a sword, that go down to the stones of the pit; as a carcass trodden under feet.

20 Thou shalt not be joined with them in burial, because thou hast destroyed thy land, *and* slain thy people: the seed of evildoers shall never be renowned.

21 Prepare slaughter for his children for the iniquity of their fathers; that they do not rise, nor possess the land, nor fill the face of the world with cities. 12Son of man, take up a lamentation upon the king of Tyrus, and say unto him, Thus saith the Lord GOD; Thou sealest up the sum, full of wisdom, and perfect in beauty.

13 Thou hast been in Eden the garden of God; every precious stone *was* thy covering, the sardius, topaz, and the diamond, the beryl, the onyx, and the jasper, the sapphire, the emerald, and the carbuncle, and gold: the workmanship of thy tabrets and of thy pipes was prepared in thee in the day that thou wast created.

14 Thou *art* the anointed cherub that covereth; and I have set thee *so*: thou wast upon the holy mountain of God; thou hast walked up and down in the midst of the stones of fire.

15 Thou *wast* perfect in thy ways from the day that thou wast created, till iniquity was found in thee.

16 By the multitude of thy merchandise they have filled the midst of thee with violence, and thou hast sinned: therefore I will cast thee as profane out of the mountain of God: and I will destroy thee, O covering cherub, from the midst of the stones of fire.

17 Thine heart was lifted up because of thy beauty, thou hast corrupted thy wisdom by reason of thy brightness: I will cast thee to the ground, I will lay thee before kings, that they may behold thee.

18 Thou hast defiled thy sanctuaries by the multitude of thine iniquities, by the iniquity of thy traffick; therefore will I bring forth a fire from the midst of thee, it shall devour thee, and I will bring thee to ashes

upon the earth in the sight of all them that behold thee.

19 All they that know thee among the people shall be astonished at thee: thou shalt be a terror, and never *shalt* thou *be* any more . Isaiah 14:12–21; Ezekiel 12–19) These passages are addressing Satan previously known as Lucifer. Lucifer, in his first estate, was beyond the supernatural in all things. He was a king and in his heart was iniquity. In the above passage, it said that Lucifer was in the garden of Eden (13Thou hast been in Eden the garden of God; every precious stone *was* thy covering, the sardius, topaz, and the diamond, the beryl, the onyx, and the jasper, the sapphire, the emerald, and the carbuncle, and gold: the workman-ship of thy tabrets and of thy pipes was prepared in thee in the day that thou wast created. Ezekiel28:13) That's not how he appeared to the woman (Eve) in the garden of Eden in Genesis (1Now the serpent was more subtil than any beast of the field which the LORD God had made. And he said unto the woman, Yea, hath God said, Ye shall not eat of every tree of the garden?

2 And the woman said unto the serpent, We may eat of the fruit of the trees of the garden:

3 But of the fruit of the tree which *is* in the midst of the garden, God hath said, Ye shall not eat of it, neither shall ye touch it, lest ye die. 4And the serpent said unto the woman, Ye shall not surely die:

5 For God doth know that in the day ye eat thereof, then your eyes shall be opened, and ye shall be as gods, knowing good and evil.

6 And when the woman saw that the tree *was* good for food, and that *it was* pleasant to the eyes, and a tree to be desired to make *one* wise, she took of the fruit thereof, and did eat, and gave also unto her husband with her; and he did eat.

7 And the eyes of them both were opened, and they knew that they *were* naked; and they sewed fig leaves together, and made themselves aprons.

8 And they heard the voice of the LORD God walking in the garden in the cool of the day: and Adam and his wife hid themselves from the presence of the LORD God amongst the trees of the garden.

9 And the LORD God called unto Adam, and said unto him, Where *art* thou? 10And he said, I heard thy voice in the garden, and I was afraid, because I *was* naked; and I hid myself.

11 And he said, Who told thee that thou *wast* naked? Hast thou eaten of the tree, whereof I commanded thee that thou shouldest not eat?

12 And the man said, The woman whom thou gavest *to be* with me, she gave me of the tree, and I did eat.

13 And the LORD God said unto the woman, What *is* this *that* thou hast done? And the woman said, The

serpent beguiled me, and I did eat. 14And the LORD God said unto the serpent, Because thou hast done this, thou *art* cursed above all cattle, and above every beast of the field; upon thy belly shalt thou go, and dust shalt thou eat all the days of thy life: 15And I will put enmity between thee and the woman, and between thy seed and her seed; it shall bruise thy head, and thou shalt bruise his heel. Genesis3:1-15) Now, which book was written first? The first five books of Moses or the prophet Ezekiel? Whose account describes Lucifer and whose testimony describes Satan the fallen cherub?

In order for a spirit, which angels are, to be adorned with the most precious gemstones of the Earth angels must be of matter i.e. flesh. Whether angels create their own flesh or God makes it for them I'm not sure. . So, Eden was on first Earth and Lucifer (not Adam and Eve) were there. Perhaps, like Adam, Lucifer had dominion over Eden, and when God recreated Eden, Satan wanted it back and deceived Eve and Adam to reclaim it. (4And the serpent said unto the woman, Ye shall not surely die:5For God doth know that in the day ye eat thereof, then your eyes shall be opened, and ye shall be as gods, knowing good and evil.

6 And when the woman saw that the tree *was* good for food, and that it *was* pleasant to the eyes, and a tree to be desired to make *one* wise, she took of the fruit thereof, and did eat, and gave also unto her husband with her; and he did eat. Genesis3:4–6.)

Lucifer's first estate was so lofty that as the anointed cherub that covereth he sat on God's high hill on top of God's holy mountain which is above heaven. Consider there is infinite outer space. Then above that is heaven. Somewhere high above that is God's holy mountain. On top of the mountain is God's holy hill. . Ascending above that hill are clouds. Transcendingly higher than the clouds somewhere is where the most high God resides. That's how close Lucifer was to God!

Iniquity was within Lucifer and the multitude of his mercantilism was filled with violence and sin i.e., he practiced these things. It is written (8He that committeth sin is of the devil; for the devil sinneth from the beginning. For this purpose the Son of God was manifested, that he might destroy the works of the devil. 44Ye are of *your* father the devil, and the lusts of your father ye will do. He was a murderer from the beginning, and abode not in the truth, because there is no truth in him. When he speaketh a lie, he speaketh of his own: for he is a liar, and the father of it. 1John3:8; John8:44)

Lucifer couldn't murder angels because angels are spirits and spirits are immortal. (13Thou shalt not kill. 12He that smiteth a man, so that he die, shall be surely put to death.

13 And if a man lie not in wait, but God deliver *him* into his hand; then I will appoint thee a place whither he shall flee.

14 But if a man come presumptuously upon his neighbour, to slay him with guile; thou shalt take him from mine altar, that he may die. 21Or in enmity smite him with his hand, that he die: he that smote *him* shall surely be put to death; *for* he *is* a murderer: the revenger of blood shall slay the murderer, when he meeteth him.

22 But if he thrust him suddenly without enmity, or have cast upon him any thing without laying of wait,

23 Or with any stone, wherewith a man may die, seeing *him* not, and cast *it* upon him, that he die, and *was* not his enemy, neither sought his harm:

24 Then the congregation shall judge between the slayer and the revenger of blood according to these judgments:

25 And the congregation shall deliver the slayer out of the hand of the revenger of blood, and the congregation shall restore him to the city of his refuge, whither he was fled: and he shall abide in it unto the death of the high priest, which was anointed with the holy oil.

26 But if the slayer shall at any time come without the border of the city of his refuge, whither he was fled;

27 And the revenger of blood find him without the borders of the city of his refuge, and the revenger of blood kill the slayer; he shall not be guilty of blood:

28 Because he should have remained in the city of his refuge until the death of the high priest: but after the death of the high priest the slayer shall return into the land of his possession.

29 So these *things* shall be for a statute of judgment unto you throughout your generations in all your dwellings.

30 Whoso killeth any person, the murderer shall be put to death by the mouth of witnesses: but one witness shall not testify against any person *to cause him* to die.

31 Moreover ye shall take no satisfaction for the life of a murderer, which *is* guilty of death: but he shall be surely put to death.

32 And ye shall take no satisfaction for him that is fled to the city of his refuge, that he should come again to dwell in the land, until the death of the priest.

33 So ye shall not pollute the land wherein ye *are*: for blood it defileth the land: and the land cannot be cleansed of the blood that is shed therein, but <u>by the blood of him that shed it.</u>

34 <u>Defile not therefore the land which ye shall inhabit, wherein I dwell: for I</u>

<u>the LORD dwell among the children of Israel.</u> Exodus 21:12–14; Numbers 35:11–34). According to the word, that is the penalty for a murderer. Satan was a sinner and a murderer from the beginning, is to imply that ever since first Earth, he was murdering mortal flesh. Murder is a premeditate act unlike a kill, which is not necessarily predetermined. Lucifer's iniquity was so evil that he was committing murder in his mind before actually executing it. This is written of him (**14**<u>Forasmuch then as</u> <u>the children are partakers of</u> <u>flesh and blood, he also himself likewise took</u> <u>part of the same; that through death he might destroy him</u> <u>that had the</u> <u>power of death, that is, the devil;</u> **28**And fear not them which kill the body, but are not able to kill the soul: but rather fear him which is able to destroy both soul and body in hell. **19**<u>But thou art cast</u> <u>out of thy grave like an</u> <u>abominable branch,</u> *and as* <u>the raiment of those that are slain, thrust</u> <u>through with</u> <u>a sword, that go down to the stones of the pit; as a carcase</u> <u>trodden under feet.</u>

20 <u>Thou shalt not be joined with them in burial, because thou hast destroyed</u> <u>thy land,</u> *and* <u>slain thy</u> <u>people: the seed of evildoers shall never be</u> <u>renowned.</u> Hebrews 2:14; Matthew 10:28; Isaiah 14:19, 20)

One eye witness that saw Satan fall from his first estate was Jesus the Christ. (**18**<u>And he said unto</u> <u>them, I beheld Satan as lightning fall from heaven.</u>Luke10:18) The bible says that Satan was reduced to ashes in the sight of all those who beheld him. (**18**<u>Thou hast defiled thy sanctuaries by the multitude of</u> <u>thine iniquities, by the iniquity of thy traffick; therefore will I bring forth a fire from the midst of thee, it</u> <u>shall devour thee, and I will bring thee to ashes upon the earth in the sight of all them that behold thee.</u> Ezekiel28:18) That could possibly imply that his flesh was burned off permanently making him a discarnate spirit. Devils can't incarnate only angels can. As in the cases of Legion and Mary Magdelene devils can only possess flesh. (**6**<u>But when he saw Jesus afar off, he ran and worshipped him,</u> **7**<u>And cried with a</u> <u>loud voice, and said, What have I to do with thee, Jesus,</u> *thou* <u>Son of</u> <u>the most high God? I adjure thee by</u> <u>God, that thou torment me not.</u>

8 <u>For he said unto him,</u> Come out of the man, *thou* unclean spirit.

9 <u>And he asked him, What</u> *is* thy name? <u>And he answered, saying, My name</u> *is* <u>Legion:</u> <u>for we are many.</u>

10 <u>And he besought him much that he would not send them away out of the country.</u>

11 <u>Now there was there nigh unto the mountains a great herd of swine feeding.</u> **12**<u>And all the devils</u> <u>besought him, saying, Send us into the swine, that we may enter</u> <u>into them.</u>

13 And forthwith Jesus gave them leave. And the unclean spirits went out, and entered into the swine: and the herd ran violently down a steep place into the sea, (they were about two thousand;) and were choked in the sea.

9 Now when *Jesus* was risen early the first *day* of the week, he appeared first to Mary Magdalene, out of whom he had cast seven devils. 2And certain women, which had been healed of evil spirits and infirmities, Mary called Magdalene, out of whom went seven devils, Mark 16:9; Luke 8:2) This one fallen angel once made nations (multitudes of people) weak! (12How art thou fallen from heaven, O Lucifer, son of the morning! *how* art thou cut down to the ground, which didst weaken the nations! Isaiah14:12)

Lucifer was so brutally tough that he made the Earth tremble and shake the kingdoms of first Earth. (16They that see thee shall narrowly look upon thee, *and* consider thee, *saying, Is* this the man that made the earth to tremble, that did shake kingdoms; Isaiah14:16) It is my opinion that Lucifer's iniquity and violence upon first Earth preceded his five count indictment

(13 For thou hast said in thine heart, I will ascend into heaven, I will exalt my throne above the stars of God: I will sit also upon the mount of the congregation, in the sides of the north:

14I will ascend above the heights of the clouds; I will be like the most High.

Isaiah 14:13, 14), which was perhaps the catalyst to him gaining one-third of the heavenly host to side with him and wage war in heaven versus the archangel Michael and his angels. (And his tail drew the third part of the stars of heaven, and did cast them to the earth: and the dragon stood before the woman which was ready to be delivered, for to devour her child as soon as it was born.

7 And there was war in heaven: Michael and his angels fought against the dragon; and the dragon fought and his angels,

8 And prevailed not; neither was their place found any more in heaven.

9 And the great dragon was cast out, that old serpent, called the Devil, and Satan, which deceiveth the whole world: he was cast out into the earth, and his angels were cast out with him.

10 And I heard a loud voice saying in heaven, Now is come salvation, and strength, and the kingdom of our God, and the power of his Christ: for the accuser of our brethren is cast down, which accused them before our God day and night. Rev12:4,7–10). Some angels that were on Lucifer's side for the rebellion ended up here. (4For if God spared not the angels that sinned, but cast *them* down to hell, and delivered *them* into chains of darkness, to be reserved unto judgment; 6And the angels which kept not their first estate, but left their own habitation, he hath reserved in everlasting chains under darkness unto the judgment

of the great day. 2Peter2:4; Jude6) Perhaps these are the angels that man will judge. (3Know ye not that we shall judge angels? how much more things that pertain to this life? 1 Corinthians 6:3)

How long did first earth exist? I'm not sure. It is safe to say that it existed long enough for kingdoms and nations to be established.

Lucifer was allowed to continue his iniquity and violence on first Earth seemingly unchecked. He was God-like on first Earth, wearing man's mortal flesh. Lucifer was flawlessly beautiful and full of wisdom. Therefore, it must have been relatively easy for him to attract, seduce, manipulate, and deceive others to do his will. (12Son of man, take up a lamentation upon the king of Tyrus, and say unto him, Thus saith the Lord GOD; Thou sealest up the sum, full of wisdom, and perfect in beauty.

14 Thou *art* the anointed cherub that covereth; and I have set thee *so*: thou wast upon the holy mountain of God; thou hast walked up and down in the midst of the stones of fire.

15 Thou *wast* perfect in thy ways from the day that thou wast created, till iniquity was found in thee.

16 By the multitude of thy merchandise they have filled the midst of thee with violence, and thou hast sinned: therefore I will cast thee as profane out of the mountain of God: and I will destroy thee, O covering cherub, from the midst of the stones of fire.

17 Thine heart was lifted up because of thy beauty, thou hast corrupted thy wisdom by reason of thy brightness: I will cast thee to the ground, I will lay thee before kings, that they may behold thee.

18 Thou hast defiled thy sanctuaries by the multitude of thine iniquities, by the iniquity of thy traffick; therefore will I bring forth a fire from the midst of thee, it shall devour thee, and I will bring thee to ashes upon the earth in the sight of all them that behold thee. 8He that committeth sin is of the devil; for the devil sinneth from the beginning. For this purpose the Son of God was manifested, that he might destroy the works of the devil. Ezekiel28:12,14-18; 1John3:8)

The Lord God Almighty created an innumerable company of angels. (22 But

Hebrews 12:22) Innumerable is the same as indeterminate. Mathematically, one-third of indeterminate can be expressed as 1/3 divided into ∞. That's awesomely mind blowing! I used one-third because Lucifer successfully persuaded one-third of God's innumerable hosts to side with him to rebel against God. (4And his tail drew the third part of the stars of heaven, and did cast them to the earth: and the dragon stood before the woman which was ready to be delivered, for to devour her child as soon as it was born. 8And prevailed not; neither was their place found any more in heaven.9And the great dragon was cast out, that old serpent, called the Devil, and Satan, which deceiveth the whole world: he was cast out into the earth, and his angels were cast out with him. Revelation 12:4, 7–9)

Satan was hurled to first Earth in the destructive form of a living lightning bolt. (18And he said unto them, I beheld Satan as lightning fall from heaven. Luke10:18) Imagine what damage that would cause? When asteroids and comets hit the planet don't, they cause damage? Doesn't lightning usually inflict destruction upon the Earth when it strikes? Now, imagine one-third of the innumerable company of fallen angels being cast out of heaven in the form of living lightning bolts. What utter destruction would they inflict upon the entire cosmos? All of this occurred prior to Genesis1:2. Genesis1:1 refers to first Earth which was destroyed by Satan's cosmic cataclysm. When Satan and his fallen angels were cast out of heaven everything under heaven was utterly devastated. God sent His Holy Spirit to inspect the damage. (2And the earth was without form, and void; and darkness was upon the face of the deep. And the Spirit of God moved upon the face of the waters. Genesis1:2) In the Bible, this is the first account of activity of The Holy Spirit of God. As it is written, the Holy Spirit was sent out prior to God restoring the face of the Earth and creation. (30Thou sendest forth thy spirit, they are created: and thou renewest the face of the earth. Psalms 104:30). Consider why planets in our solar system have no life. Most are dead planets, uninhabitable moons, etc. The universe is groaning in a state of decay awaiting the children of God to liberate it. (22For we know that the whole creation groaneth and travaileth in pain together until now. Romans 8:22)

God created first Earth and the heavens, shook them, then recreated second, or present Earth as we know it. (1In the beginning God created the heaven and the earth. 13Therefore I will shake the heavens, and the earth shall remove out of her place, in the wrath of the LORD of hosts, and in the day of his fierce anger.

26Whose voice then shook the earth: but now he hath promised, saying, Yet once more I shake not the earth only, but also heaven.

27 And this word, Yet once more, signifieth the removing of those things that are shaken, as of things that are made, that those things which cannot be shaken may remain. Genesis1.1; Isaiah13:13; Hebrews12:26,27)

Satan was responsible for desecrating the holiness of heaven and causing the cosmic cataclysm. It's important to note that God didn't recreate anything until He the Holy Spirit first moved into action. (2And the earth was without form, and void; and darkness was upon the face of the deep. And the Spirit of God moved upon the face of the waters. Genesis1:2(30Thou sendest forth thy spirit, they are created: and thou renewest the face of the earth. Psalms 104:30). The Holy Spirit is so vitally important in all things that it is written (**6**<u>Then he answered and spake unto me, saying, This *is* the word of the LORD unto Zerubbabel,</u> <u>saying, Not by might, nor by power, but by my spirit, saith the LORD of hosts.</u> **29**But he that shall blaspheme against the Holy Ghost hath never forgiveness, but is in danger of eternal damnation: Zecariah 4:6; Mark 3:29). After the Lord restored creation, Satan deceived Eve and Adam and stole their dominion of second Earth from them. Lucifer was debased from his first estate as the anointed cherubim that covereth to Satan the Devil, The Prince of this world which is second Earth (**31**Now is the judgment of this world: now shall the prince of this world be cast out. "Wherein in time past ye walked according to the course of this world, according to the prince of the power of the air, the spirit that now worketh in the children of disobedience" John 12:31; Ephesians 2:2)

God is not a god of disorder (**33**<u>For God is not</u> *the author* <u>of confusion, but of peace, as in all churches</u> <u>of the saints.</u> 1Corinthians14:33) He assigned ranks to his heavenly hosts (**21**<u>And it shall come to pass in</u> <u>that day,</u> *that* <u>the LORD shall punish the host of the high ones</u> *that are* <u>on high, and the kings of the earth</u> <u>upon the earth.</u> **20**<u>And are built upon the foundation of the apostles and prophets, Jesus Christ himself</u> <u>being the chief corner</u> *stone*; "To the intent that now unto the principalities and powers in heavenly *places* might be known by the church the manifold wisdom of God, Isaiah24:21,22; Ephesians2:20;3:10) The jurisdiction of a prince is his princedom also known as his principality. It is unclear whether the angel Michael had the title of the Archangel prior to Lucifer's fall. What is clear is that in (Revelation12:7 **7**<u>And there was war in heaven: Michael and his angels fought against the dragon; and the</u> <u>dragon fought and his angels,</u>) he is merely referred to as Michael. He has the uniquely distinctive title of the Archangel in (<u>Yet Michael the archangel, when contending with the devil he disputed about the body</u> <u>of Moses, durst not bring against him a railing accusation, but said, The Lord rebuke thee.</u> Jude1:9)

The Archangel Michael is one of the chief princes in the spiritual world. (**13** <u>But the prince of the king-</u> <u>dom of Persia withstood me one and twenty days: but, lo, Michael, one of the chief princes, came to help</u> <u>me; and I remained there with the kings of Persia.</u> Daniel10:13) Michael's principality/princedom is Israel. There are other princes mentioned in the Bible such as **20** <u>Then said he, Knowest thou wherefore</u> <u>I come</u> <u>unto thee? and now will I return to fight with the prince of Persia: and when I am gone forth, lo, the prince</u> <u>of Grecia shall come.</u> **2** <u>Son of man, set thy face against Gog, the land of Magog, the chief prince of Meshech</u> <u>and Tubal, and prophesy against him,</u> **3** <u>And say, Thus saith the Lord GOD; Behold, I</u> *am* <u>against thee, O</u> <u>Gog, the chief prince of Meshech and Tubal:</u> **25** <u>And through his policy also he shall cause craft to prosper</u>

in his hand; and he shall magnify *himself* in his heart, and by peace shall destroy many: he shall also stand up against the Prince of princes; but he shall be broken without hand. Daniel 10:20; Ezekiel 38:2,3; Daniel 8:25. It is my belief that the term principalities, which is usually written in a plural tense, also means princes, a ranking of angels. Oftentimes, the term principalities is mentioned before powers (12 For we wrestle not against flesh and blood, but against principalities, against powers, against the rulers of the darkness of this world, against spiritual wickedness in high *places.* 10And ye are complete in him, which is the head of all principality and power: 15 *And* having spoiled principalities and powers, he made a shew of them openly, triumphing over them in it. 16 For by him were all things created, that are in heaven, and that are in earth, visible and invisible, whether *they be* thrones, or dominions, or principalities, or powers: all things were created by him, and for him: 1 Put them in mind to be subject to principalities and powers, to obey magistrates, to be ready to every good work, Ephesians 6:12; Colossians 1:16, 2:10,15; Titus 3:1)

The blessed hope is going to be the introduction to third Earth. (But the day of the Lord will come as a thief in the night; in the which the heavens shall pass away with a great noise, and the elements shall melt with fervent heat, the earth also and the works that are therein shall be burned up.

11 *Seeing* then *that* all these things shall be dissolved, what manner *of persons* ought ye to be in *all* holy conversation and godliness,

12 Looking for and hasting unto the coming of the day of God, wherein the heavens being on fire shall be dissolved, and the elements shall melt with fervent heat?

13 Nevertheless we, according to his promise, look for new heavens and a new earth, wherein dwelleth righteousness. And I saw a new heaven and a new earth: for the first heaven and the first earth were passed away; and there was no more sea. And he that sat upon the throne said, Behold, I make all things new. And he said unto me, Write: for these words are true and faithful. 2Peter3:10-13; Revelation21:1;5). According to the word creation as we know it will be destroyed and made new. It is my opinion that the saints will be commissioned by God to replenish third Earth as well as taking part in the restoration of other planets. I hope that the evidence I presented to you, my readership, has proven to be incisive. Thank-you and God bless you all.

Sincerely, Ivor Forbes

References: https://www.kingjamesbibleonline.org/Genesis-Chapter-1/.

www.ingramcontent.com/pod-product-compliance
Lightning Source LLC
Chambersburg PA
CBHW040200110726
48005CB00018B/2836